OLATUNJI OLUBAYO

THE

POWER

OF

DIVINE

PURPOSE

*Discover what it takes to live life to the
FULLEST, as you lay hold on God's
ORIGINAL INTENTION
For your life*

The Power of Divine Purpose
by Olatunji Oluibayo

ISBN: 978-978-917-847-6

Published by
EXCEL PUBLISHING HOUSE
...Publishing the mission with Passion
(An arm of souls Aflame Ministries International)
+234-802-959-1841; 234-803-474-3878; 234-809-859-1841
Email: sam_intl2002@yahoo.co.uk
Website: www.soulsaflame.org

Produced by
Stay Alive Int'l
Beseech Concepts: 11, Olowu Street, Ikeja, Lagos
stayaliveintl@gmail.com +234 809 822 0369, 802 930 9859

Unless otherwise stated, scriptural quotations are from the New King James Version of the Holy Bible, copyright 1979, 1980, 1982, 1988, Thomas Nelson Inc.
Scriptures marked MSG are from the Message Translation.
Scriptures marked GNT are from the Good News Translation.

DEDICATION

To the loving memory of my late father, *Sylvester Olufemi Shobayo (1943-1995)*. And to my mother, *Margaret Otiti Shobayo..* They paid the price to ensure that I and my siblings get the best start in life.

Also to everyone in search of God's perfect will for their lives, and to those on the path of purpose.

May the lord grant you fulfilment in life and Ministry as you lay hold tenaciously on the POWER OF DIVINE PURPOSE

ACKNOWLEDGMENT

I t is ten years since the Lord gave me the inspiration to put into writing what you hold in your hands today. Since then, my life has been positively impacted by many purpose driven people. Space will not permit an accurate or detailed list of each person's significance in my life and to the successful authorship of this book.

My special appreciation goes to Dr Hugh Osgood for his fatherly counsel at my moments of transition and also for writing the foreword to this book; Rev Dr. D.K Aboderin for his guidance and encouragement over the years; Apostle Tom Samson who by precept and example taught me how not to give up on one's dream; Rev Dr. Bisi Afolayan for giving me a chance to prove my ministry, and Apostle Victor Uchegbulam for motivating me both to lead and impart leadership principles unto others.

A big thank you to all my mentors, big brothers and covenant friends: Pastor Tony Olukoyede, Rev Tony Akinyemi, Pastor Peter and Becky Onuarunmhi, Rev and Dr Mrs Duro-Aina, Pastor Martins Fatola, Rev and Rev (Mrs) Ola-kris Akinola, Pastor Israel Tokunbo Emmanuel, Pastor Evans Adetokunbo Emmanuel, Pastor

Nnamdi Dan-Ayam, Rev Best Ozuligbo, Bishop Dr Collins Ogunlade.

Thanks to all my friends, partners, and protégés too numerous to mention. Your input to my life and to the timely release of this book will not go unrewarded.

I cannot forget the selfless contribution of Evangelist David Eniola Opeyemi to the publishing of this book, and many thanks to Charles Ozuligbo for his professional touch in proof reading the typescript.

To the entire membership of Eternal Glory Assembly International Church, thanks for giving me the privilege of learning firsthand the principles of true leadership.

I am deeply indebted to my lovely wife, a treasure of inestimable value. Thanks for supporting the fulfilment of my uncommon purpose. And to David and Vanessa, I love you so much, thanks for believing absolutely in daddy's divine assignment.

Most of all, to the God and Father of our Lord Jesus Christ, the God of PURPOSE, be honour, glory, and praise for making this book a reality.
- Olatunji Olubayo

CONTENTS

HEAR WHAT OTHERS SAY

"In the book- **THE POWER OF DIVINE PURPOSE**, the Reverend Tunji Shobayo delves into the dimensions of understanding required to both discover and fulfill one's purpose in life. He not only expounds on the futility of a purposeless life, he also goes a step further by stipulating quite unequivocally and in no uncertain terms, how to discover and fulfill purpose. Reading the manuscript has been a tremendous blessing to me. I wish I could put a copy of this book in the hands of every young person seeking to find their feet in life".

- Rev Tony Akinyemi
(Senior Pastor-The Shepherd's Flock International Church, Ikeja, Lagos)

"I know Pastor Tunji to be a person of purpose and conviction - godly attributes that shine through the pages of his new book. How I wish more people in the Church will lay all aside and pursue the true reason for their existence like he has!
THE POWER OF DIVINE PURPOSE will surely stir you in the right direction."

- Pastor Israel Adetokunbo Emmanuel
(International Director of Books with a Mission& founder of The Writers' Well UK).

"**THE POWER OF DIVINE PURPOSE** is a timely reawakening to the subject of purpose in a world where people are being distracted by all manners of threats to their existence by terrorism, economic downturn, natural disasters and other socio-political disorders of our time.

Pastor Tunji Olubayo in his characteristic energetic manner of projecting the truth of God's word brings us back from our distractions to thinking on the reason why we must survive and ultimately, on the power for our survival: The Power of Divine Purpose. We *only* exist to discover and pursue *divine* purpose and when we lay hold on it, it keeps us alive Luke 13:6-9, John 7:30. Everyone should read this book to develop resilience in these days of deadly distractions."
- Rev Evans Adetokunbo Emmanuel
(Grace Mission International, Lagos Nigeria).

"Some people write better than they live; others live better than they write. Pastor Tunji, there's no disparity between your life and the content of this book-
THE POWER OF DIVINE PURPOSE.

Life without Purpose is a burden. This book will raise the readers from the common place of life and establish them among the fulfilled as they apply the secrets expounded in it.

This book will indeed kindle a fresh fire in the hearts of the readers. Destinies will be transformed when they lay hold on this book. It is truly inspiring and awesome. I strongly recommend it."
- Pastor Martins Fatola *(Senior Pastor& Author, cutting Edge Word ministries International Canada)*

"A must read for everyone that wants to make a mark in life. The author has contributed a considerable quota in making people operate right in the centre of God's will for their lives. This is a *MUST READ!*"
- Pastor Tony Olukoyede *(Senior Pastor His Purpose Church Agidingbi, Lagos)*

"This book, ***"THE POWER OF DIVINE PURPOSE"*** has tremendously blessed my heart and I believe it will bless yours too. It sets a basic foundation for a purposeful living."
- Rev Dr. D. k. Aboderin *(Author & Senior Pastor Faith Family Bible Church Ojodu-Lagos).*

"On every page his passion is there to inspire us... and inspire us he most certainly does! You will not be able to read this book and stay unchallenged and unchanged."
Dr Hugh Osgood *(Founder and President Churches in Communities International)*

FOREWORD

Rev Olatunji Olubayo has done us a great service by gathering together so much powerful material to push us forward in pursuit of THE POWER OF DIVINE PURPOSE.

On every page his passion is there to inspire us... and inspire us he most certainly does! You will not be able to read this book and stay unchallenged and unchanged.

I have known Olatunji Olubayo for some years now and have seen at close quarters the quality of his life and ministry.

As you draw on what he has written, you will not only tap into his passion but into his integrity. Passion and integrity need to go hand-in-hand in pursuit of THE POWER OF DIVINE PURPOSE. May God truly transform your life as you read.

-Dr Hugh Osgood,
Founder and President, Churches in Communities International.

INTRODUCTION

The most effective deployment of any creation can best be described by the Originator. Our lives have an origin. And it is in that original crafting that the reason for existence is hidden. While we create our values and pursue our goals, we need to be reminded that such drives in life are just a means to an end. Every phase of our lives is a process towards a clearly pre-determined end.

And until we understand our purposes, everything we do will not make a meaning. And when we force a wrong thought on our minds, believing in the wrong pursuits, we eventually feel unfulfilled inside us.

To live a successful life, we need to return to the Author of life. He has an intention that is very original and specific to each life He crafted. The wisdom to search that truth that brings inner fulfillment is what this book inspires. It will definitely move you from the pursuance of things to fulfillment in life. And just in case you have tried your best and still feel helpless, *read through the entire pages again.* It contains exciting solutions to getting beyond challenges and arriving at the very essence of your existence.

The inspiration this book offers will ignite the passion in you to maximize your purpose for living and remain on course. Even where you are already privileged to know your purpose for living, this book offers further clarifications and insights to sharpen your focus and enhance your successful attainment. Whether you are discovering it or you are releasing it, take advantage of these insights to maximize it.

You are not a biological accident. You were crafted with an intention in the mind of the Creator. Engage that drive and move on to a life of fulfillment.
Soar!

-Steve Akoni
Senior Pastor- First Assembly, Ogba- Lagos.

AUTHOR'S PREFACE

artin Luther King Jr. said, **"If a man hasn't discovered something that he will die for, he isn't fit to live"**[1]. That means until a man discovers the essence of his existence, he can only be considered a "living corpse", merely existing and not living.

Therefore, the discovery of purpose becomes a non-negotiable part of our journey through life.

The essence of this book goes beyond the excitement that comes from information received. Rather, it is sent to "provoke" those that are ignorant of God's purpose for their lives, thereby igniting their faith, both to pursue and fulfill their God ordained purpose.

Those already on the path of purpose are not left out; for their pursuit of purpose is enhanced as they take an adventure through the pages of this book. Many with abandoned dreams would be inspired to pick it up, as they continue in the race towards DESTINY.

- Olatunji Olubayo

PROLOGUE

Washington Irving once said: **"Great minds have purposes, others have wishes"**[1], some are *"Visionaries"* while others are *"Wishionaries"*. To what category do you belong? Great minds do not only have great purposes but they accomplish great feats. They discover their God ordained purpose and pursue it, thereby fulfilling their destinies.

Friend, every man is sent to the earth with a definite purpose or assignment to fulfill. Your purpose has the power or capacity to make you great, and this fact is the foundation upon which true success is achieved, for God's purpose for your life is the yardstick by which He rates your performance.

Therefore, a man that does not discover his purpose merely exists. He will pass through the world, but will leave no footprints on the sands of time.

It is sad that many in our generation are less concerned about their need to discover or pursue their God ordained purpose; they end up living a life patterned and directed by their environment. They get entangled in the routine–like drama played out by this present generation, being oblivious of God's divine purpose for their lives. They become unfulfilled, without satisfaction, settling down to a life that may be generally acceptable by all and sundry but falling short of God's original intention.

Therefore, it's highly essential for us to discover God's original intention for our lives. This discovery holds the key to the release of our abilities, gifts, talents and potentials.

Every manufacturer makes his products based on his intention or purpose for it and he puts in place everything needed for it to fulfill its assignment.

Similarly, we have been packaged by God to fulfill a certain assignment which cannot be limited by who we are, where we were born, who our parents were, etc. His purpose for our lives is no respecter of colour, race, academic qualification or profession; rather, it has the power to shape our lives, our society and our generation[2].

Therefore, it is highly imperative that we discover God's purpose for our lives as we lay hold on the "POWER OF DIVINE PURPOSE"

- Olatunji Olubayo

*I know what I'm doing.
I have it all planned out.
Plans to take care of you,
not abandon you, plans to give
you the future you hope for.*

(Jeremiah 29:11 MSG)

THE GOD OF PURPOSE

Every manufacturer makes his products based on his predetermined intention. Therefore, God like any other manufacturer operated on the platform of purpose. The purposeful steps taken by God in the book of Genesis reveals the meticulous arrangement of God's creation.

Everything made at creation through God's word was not only a plus on the previous but every preceding step had an assignment towards the next step. Everything God made had a definite purpose for its creation.

➤ *Then God said, "let there be light"; and there was light - Genesis 1:3*

➤ *Then God said, "let the earth bring forth grass, the herb that yields seed, and the fruit tree that yields fruit according to its kind, whose seed is in itself, on the earth"; and it was so - Genesis 1:11*

➢ ***Then God said, "let the earth bring forth the living creature according to its kind: cattle and creeping things and the beast of the earth, each according to its kind"; and it was so - Genesis 1:24***

God made the light to sustain the growth of the plants. Plants on the otherhand require light for food production through the process of photosynthesis[1].

The assignment of the light was for the sustenance of the plants, and God, driven by purpose made sure that plants never came on the scene before the light was put in place. God also, did not bring forth living creatures until He had put in place the light and the plants that would be needed for their survival.

Finally, He formed man out of the dust of the earth, whose survival depends on plants for oxygen and for food, and the plants on the other hand depended on light for their survival. With every step in creation, God had a purpose of what he wanted to achieve.

His purpose was the driving force behind His "Creative Ability". Thus, we can say, His purpose released His "Creative Potential". The best of God was expressed when His *PURPOSE* was *PURSUED*. Until purpose is discovered and pursued, potential remains untapped.

YOU ARE PURPOSE ORIENTED

The Bible reveals that man was created in God's own image and likeness[2]. God's intention was not only for men (that includes the women folk) to be like Him, but beyond this, He wanted man to act like Him, because the earth according to God's purpose was to be an extension of Heaven, a colony of the kingdom of Heaven.

Man was commissioned by God to rule on His behalf in the earth. His commissioning was established with five primary purposes to be fulfilled.

Then God blessed them, and God said to them, be fruitful and multiply; fill the earth and subdue it; have dominion over the fish of the sea, and over the birds of the air, and over every living thing that moves on the earth. - Genesis 1:28

God blessed them (the first man and woman), imparting on them the potential for *fruitfulness, multiplication* and the ability to *fill the earth, subdue* and *dominate* their world.

Little wonder, that the first man (Adam) had such inherent ability to conduct a worldwide naming ceremony exercise for every beast of the field and every fowl of the air[3].

> **Until purpose is discovered and pursued, potentials remains untapped!**

The first man was introduced to the earth with a clear cut purpose, hence no one, traced from the linage of Adam, can gain access to this world without an established purpose from God. Eve herself, was not brought to the scene until God had clearly defined her purpose.

God said.... ***"It is not good that a man should be alone; I will (manufacture for) him a help meet (or suitable) for him"*** ***(Genesis 2:18).***

Eve was a solution to the solitary life Adam had to live in the garden. Though he was not lonely as some say, because he enjoyed God's presence, but he needed a companion of his own kind.

Therefore, God pulled Eve out of him, to help him accomplish his purpose[4]. Your purpose therefore is the solution to other people's problems; it is designed to answer the question of another.

The God of purpose through the power of His purpose shaped the first world which was void and dark that He might "manufacture" sons of purpose who will use the same power to shape their world.

Friend, it is time to wake up to the reality that we are creatures of purpose, sent to the world on a mission to accomplish a specific assignment assigned to us by God. It is our commitment to this course that brings lasting Joy, satisfaction and fulfillment.

In the words of John Marm Brown: **"life owes us little; we owe it everything. The only true happiness comes from squandering ourselves for a "PURPOSE".**

> **The God of purpose through the power of His purpose shaped the first world which was void and dark, that He might "manufacture" sons of purpose who will use the same power to shape their world.**

It is high time; we put in all we have got in the pursuance of our God ordained purpose as we seek tenaciously the "GOD OF PURPOSE".

CHAPTER ONE-SUMMARY

***The God of purpose*:**

1. Right from creation God was purposeful in all His actions, and everything He made had a definite Purpose for its creation.

2. Every creation of God had a definite assignment towards the next one.

3. God's creative potential at the beginning of creation was a product of His Purpose.

4. The best of God was expressed when His purpose was pursued.

You are purpose Oriented:

1. God's desire was not only for man to look like Him, but also to act like Him

2. The first man was introduced into the earth with a clear cut assignment; hence no man gains access into the earth without an established purpose.

3. It is time we put all our energy into the pursuit of our God ordained purpose.

REFLECTIONS

1.   Can I really say that I've been living a purposeful life?

2.   Do I approach each day of my life with a definite purpose in mind?

3.   With a close look at my life, how much of God do I reflect?

4.   Do I have any clue to what my divine Purpose in life should be; if yes, am I pursuing it's fulfillment with all my heart?

*The fullness or emptiness of life
will be measured by the extent to
which a man feels that he has an
impact on the lives of others.
To be a man is to matter to someone
outside you, or to some calling
or cause bigger than you.*

- Kingman Brewster

GET ACQUAINTED WITH YOUR PURPOSE

The purpose of anything is the essence for its existence. It is the reason why any product is manufactured. It is the intention of the maker for creating a product. Therefore, it becomes essential to understand the very purpose of a thing for this will determine its usefulness. A life without an understanding of purpose is a "useless life".

The purpose of any product can only be discovered by contacting the manufacturer, for he knows the intricate details about the product, its strengths, weakness, abilities or potentials. He also knows to what capacity the product will best perform.

Your friends, colleagues, associates, parents, family, children and mentors cannot determine your purpose. Only the manufacturer has the sole prerogative to do so. God is your manufacturer, your creator, your source and your maker. Your contact with Him will open up to you your life given mission on earth.

Understand that your accomplishment in life or the wealth you have acquired is not a guarantee that your purpose has been accomplished.

Many successful people according to the world's standards, have ended up living a life without fulfillment or satisfaction, a life of confusion and emptiness, some were even reported to have committed suicide at the peak of their success. They all had one thing in common, they pursued goals that gave them neither joy nor fulfillment and they continually wondered why this was so.

Take note, that success has no meaning and accomplishment has no satisfaction without purpose, for the discovery of purpose is the key to a fulfilling life.

PURPOSE DEFINED

1.   The purpose of a thing is the manufacturer's **"Original Intention"** for its

production. **And *we know that all things work together for good to those who love God, to those who are the called according to His purpose[1].***

The word "purpose" used in this verse of scripture, actually means "Original Intention". What a joy to know that God has a specific intention for your creation, your confusion though notwithstanding.

There is a reason for your existence. You might have tried to fit in, but to no avail; you might have been ostracized; set aside by friends and family, not being accepted in the club or clique. Welcome on board, I have been there too. You need to know that you were not created by God to *"BLEND IN"* rather you were made to *"STAND OUT"*.

You are special, and unique; a creature of great significance, to be celebrated and not tolerated. There are no two kinds of you on earth. You are a rare breed, because God has a specific intention for your life.

Scientists tells us that no two humans on earth have the same fingerprint or dentition, so you see, you were actually created to accomplish a special assignment, which presently you might not be pursuing but originally had been the intention of your maker.

2.   Purpose is the **essence or reason** for living.
The Bible tells us in 1 John 3:8b: *For this purpose (reason), the son of God was manifested that he might destroy the works of the devil.*

And Jesus reading from the book of the prophet Isaiah gave a detailed account of the essence of his anointing: *The spirit of the Lord is upon me, because He has anointed me to preach the gospel to the poor: he has sent me to heal the broken hearted, to proclaim liberty to the captives. And recovery of sight to the blind, to set at liberty those who are oppressed; to proclaim the acceptable year of the Lord. (Luke 4:18-19).*

Therefore, the reason why you were created is hidden in the realization of God's purpose for your life.

3.   Purpose also means **WHY?** If only you will pause and ask the question "why". This question will help you deal with the issue of purpose. For instance:

- Why am I doing what am doing presently?
- Why am I where I am now?
- Why am I living where I am living?
- Why was I born in the family that I came from?
- Etc.

We can go on and on. The question "why" forces you to deal with the issue of purpose, because the WHY of a thing determines its use, so also the WHY of a life determines its usefulness and the extent of its use. Also, it determines the willingness of a life to be used when the knowledge of "why" is contacted.

4.   Purpose is your **Assignment.**
Every man is assigned to an assignment. Your assignment provokes your *potentials*; these are innate abilities which are given by God to everyman for the fulfillment of his God given task.

Your potentials may differ from mine because we were assigned by God to different assignments. Take note, your potentials will remain buried until you step into the arena of your assignment.

5.   Purpose is the **finished desire** before you begin.
Before I formed you in the womb I knew

you; before you were born I sanctified you; I ordained you a prophet to the nations. Jeremiah 1:5

Your potentials will remain buried until you step into the arena of your assignment.

This speaks of a concluded future before the very beginning, for purpose is a predetermined destiny. God who declares the end from the beginning[2] has fixed a glorious end for you[3]. Now, He is waiting for you to discover and pursue it.

WHEN PURPOSE IS NOT DISCOVERED

Dr Myles Munroe in his book, In pursuit of purpose says: **"Ignorance of purpose leads to abuse"**.

The word abuse comes from two English words: Abnormal and use. When you are ignorant over the purpose of anything you end up using it abnormally.

The chaotic state of the world today comes from the various abuses going on around.

Everything is being abnormally used and everyone is abnormally using one another; and they also, are abnormally using themselves.

If you don't understand the purpose of a child, you will abuse the child; this is called "child abuse". Many in the world today don't know the purpose of sex, so they abuse it.

That is why fornication, adultery, homosexuality with lesbianism prevail in our society and are rampant even in the church today[4]. Whenever purpose is not discovered abuse is inevitable.

REASONS WHY PURPOSE SHOULD BE DISCOVERED.

(I). **Purpose when discovered builds confidence and determination**:

In Act 21: 10 -14, we read about the confidence and determination displayed by Paul the apostle, despite the prophetic assertions of a seasoned prophet called Agabus. Who prophesied by the Holy Ghost that Paul would be bound and delivered to the gentiles in Jerusalem; even though, the church pleaded with him not to make the journey to Jerusalem, he stuck to his decision to go, because, he had earlier received from the Lord the purpose for his journey to Jerusalem[5].

Men like Martin Luther King Junior, Nelson Mandela, Abraham Lincoln defied all odds, they withstood terrible oppositions to achieve their dreams because they laid hold on the power of divine purpose.

(ii) **Purpose when discovered guarantees focus**:

Focus is the ability to concentrate on a specific goal in order to bring about its realization. Purpose on the other hand helps you to focus on a specific goal.

Purpose makes you a man or woman of "ONE THING"- having a particular drive[6]. It stream lines your pursuits and decisions in life, it also determines where you go, what and who you listen to, the kind of friends you keep etc. It ultimately determines the direction of your life.

(iii) **Purpose when discovered reduces frustration**:

It is interesting to understand that your purpose reveals your destination. There is nothing as frustrating as initiating a journey without a clear cut understanding of your destination.

If you don't know where you are going, you will likely end up at any where. Until purpose is discovered frustration is inevitable.

(iv). **Purpose discovered establishes Cooperation**:
The discovery and pursuit of purpose automatically turns a man into a living magnet.

Napoleon Hill said: **"The moment you commit (***to a purpose***) and quit holding back, all sorts of unforeseen incidents, meetings and material assistance will rise up to help you"**.

David, after being anointed for a purpose, to be the next king of Israel, became a living magnet as he fled from King Saul into the cave Adullam[7].

Note that less privileged men were attracted to him, and these men later became great generals in his army for the establishment of his purpose as the greatest king of Israel.

The singular act of commitment to a purpose is a powerful magnet for help.

(v). **Purpose when discovered helps Assessment**:
Purpose is like a map that leads you to your

destination. Without your map, your degree of progress towards your destination will be impossible to measure.

Therefore, purpose becomes the yardstick to determine how far you have gone, or how well you are doing.

No human accolade, compliment or public applause is sufficient for an assessment in life; nothing acquired, accomplished or achieved can give a true assessment except the blue print of the Creator[8].

(vi). **Purpose when discovered eradicates Confusion**:
Confusion is as a result of broken focus. Focus is only maintained by the discovery and tenacious pursuit of purpose[9]. Whenever purpose is discovered, confusion is totally eradicated.

(vii). **Purpose when discovered gives Contentment**:
Contentment births satisfaction; which is an antidote for covetousness.

Covetousness occurs when we have a wrong definition of success or when our understanding of success is drawn from the acquisition of material possession, and not from the fulfillment of our God-given objectives.

We are to allow God's original intention for our lives to become the driving force as we live our lives in respect to money and material possession[10].

(viii). **Purpose when discovered Produces Perseverance**:
Importantly, perseverance is a virtue that can only be generated from a clear insight into what lies at the end of a challenge, struggle, pain or difficulty, experienced in the pursuit of a goal.

The Master endured untold suffering to the point of death, because He had a revelation of His purpose while on earth, therefore the end result of His suffering became glorious[11]

(ix). **Purpose when discovered confers God`s Protection**:
God says: ***And I am watching to see that my word comes true (Jeremiah 1:12 GNT)***.

Every divine purpose is revealed via God`s eternal word, and God jealously sees to it that both his word and the carrier of his word are preserved till its fulfillment.

(x). **Purpose when discovered produces Peace**:
Purpose when discovered births peace, because it eradicates confusion, ambiguity and establishes clarity.

(xi). Purpose when discovered births Passion and Commitment:
Nothing motivates a person more than a clear cut insight into the original plan, purpose or assignment for his or her life.[12]

(xii).Purpose when discovered births Success:
Bill Cosby once said: **"I don't know the key to success, but the key to failure is trying to please everybody".**

> **Success can only be truly interpreted when God's original intention for your life is been achieved**

Discovering your purpose allows you to be yourself, not trying to please everybody but doing your best to fulfill all that you were ordained to be in God.

Understand that success can only be truly interpreted when God's original intention for your life is being achieved.

(xiii).Purpose when discovered births fulfillment:
Until purpose is discovered and passionately pursued, there will be no meaning to life, for purpose is the source of fulfillment in life.

GOD'S THINKING PATTERN

Purpose determines God's action. In other words, God only acts based on His purpose[13], for God thinks in terms of purpose.

When you understand a man's thought-pattern, it is easy to determine his actions. That is why some of God's acts are misinterpreted or misunderstood by many, because it does not agree with their own plans[14].

Attitude they say determines altitude[15]. God's attitude is based on His purpose. Until you discover His attitude concerning you (i.e. Gods thinking-pattern for you) and align yourself to it, you will not rise to the level He had already prepared as your destiny.

CHAPTER TWO- SUMMARY
Get acquainted with your Purpose
1.   It is the original intention of your maker
2.   It is the essence or reason for your living
3.   It is the "WHY" of your life- The question Why helps you to deal with Purpose.
4.   It is your Assignment

5. It is God's finished desire concerning you even before you were born.

- Ignorance of purpose always leads to abuse.

Reasons why Purpose should be discovered

1. It builds confidence and determination.
2. It guarantees focus.
3. It reduces frustration.
4. It establishes co-operation.
5. It helps assessment.
6. It eradicates confusion.
7. It gives contentment.
8. It produces perseverance.
9. It confers God's protection.
0. It produces peace.
11. It births passion and commitment.
12. It births success.
13. It births fulfillment.

- God's action can only be interpreted by understanding His thinking pattern, and His thinking pattern is based solely on His purpose.

REFLECTIONS

1. A life without an understanding of purpose is a useless life, so, how useful has my life been?
2. Take time to ask yourself the following questions

a. Why am I doing what am doing presently?
b. Why am I where I am now?
c. Why am I living where am living?
d. Why was I born into the family that I came from? Etc.

3. What difference will the discovery of purpose make in my life?

4. What do I consider as the real source of fulfillment in life?

*To remove your purpose is to
significantly change
who you are, because your
purpose both informs
and reveals your nature and
responsibilities.
Everything you naturally have
and inherently are,
is necessary for you to fulfill
your purpose.
Your height, race, skin colour,
language, physical features
and intellectual capacity are all
designed for your PURPOSE.*
- Myles Munroe (1992)

3

THE ATTRIBUTES OF PURPOSE

➢ **Purpose is Divine**

Oh yes, you shaped me first inside, and then out; you formed me in my mother's womb. I thank you, High God-you're breathtaking! Body and soul I am marvelously made! I worship in adoration – what a creation! You know me inside out, you know every bone in my body; you know exactly how I was made, bit by bit, how I was sculpted from nothing into something. Like an open book, you watched me grow from conception to birth; all the STAGES OF MY LIFE were spread out before you, "<u>the days of my life all prepared before I'd even lived one day</u>". (Psalm 139: 13-16 MSG-emphasis mine)

Understand that your birth was no MISTAKE. Even if your parents never planned you, God did. Long before you were conceived by your parents you were conceived in the mind of God.

He made you for a reason, nothing in your life is arbitrary, your past defeats, regrets, disappointments or mistakes notwithstanding. He planned them all for His DIVINE PURPOSE[1].

➢ **Purpose is Unique**: God prescribed every single detail of your body. He deliberately chose your race, the color of your skin, your hair and every other feature. He also determined the natural talents or gifts you would possess and the uniqueness of your personality.

All these is intended to make you fit perfectly into that unique assignment that He assigned to you before you were born. So don't try to be like someone else, for the best you'll be is second best.

In the words of Charles Swindoll… **"There is only one you. God wanted you to be you. Don't you dare change just because you are outnumbered"**.

➢ **Purposes are interrelated**: You are created to compliment not to compete. No one is meant to be an island. You will need the purposes of others to enhance or fulfill your Purpose. Jesus, the Messiah, needed the purpose of John the Baptist as a forerunner to introduce his ministry[2].

> **There is only one you. God wanted you to be you. Don't change just because you are outnumbered!**

Your purpose is just a piece in the puzzle; but when our purposes come together we can then see the big picture.

➢ **Purpose is inherent**: God has packaged you even before conception with all that it takes to fulfill your purpose in life. Stop being envious of what someone else has that you really wish you had. The truth is that you don't need it.

Concentrate on what you have. For all it takes to be that special person God intends you to be has been built into you.

PRINCIPLES OF DIVINE PURPOSE

"There are many plans in a man's heart. Nevertheless the Lord's counsel (or purpose) that will stand" (establish or prevails) - Proverbs 19:21

"Declaring the end from beginning and from ancient times things that are not yet done. Saying, 'my counsel (purpose) shall stand, and I will do all my pleasure,' Calling a bird of prey from the east, the man who executes my counsel (or purpose), from a far country. Indeed I have spoken it; I will also bring it to pass. I have purposed it; I will also do it"
- Isaiah 46:10-11

The following principles can be derived from the scripture above.

1. Divine purpose should not be mistaken for man's plans.[3]
2. Divine purpose is specific; man's plans are many.[4]
3. Divine purpose is more important than man's plans.[5]
4. Divine purpose is more powerful than man's plans.[6]
5. Divine purpose precedes or comes before man's plans.[7]

6. God is not committed to man's plans; He is only committed and motivated by his purpose for your life.[8]

7. Man's plans are to be produced by divine purpose.[9]

8. Divine purpose does not change rather you have to change to accommodate it, and if you refuse, it can change you.[10]

9. Divine purpose is carried out through divine partnership[11]...Your purpose cannot be isolated; you will need the purposes of others to enhance or fulfill your purpose...

10. Divine purpose provokes divine provision.[12]

11. Divine purpose when discovered and pursued releases God's potentials.

12. Divine purpose gives meaning to life and it is the key to lasting fulfillment and satisfaction.

13. Divine purpose can keep one alive, for God's purpose for our lives guarantees divine protection and preservation.[13]

14. With every divine purpose comes persecutions, but persecution or oppositions are the spring board for divine promotions.

15. Divine purpose when discovered leads to divine mission.[14]

16. The effect of divine purpose lasts for generations. The world feels the impact of the mission of Christ until now.

17. Divine purpose can definitely be

transferred[15]. Beware: Every purpose not "*ACTIONED*" will be "*AUCTIONED*".

18. Divine purpose puts you in a class of your own, because it reveals your uniqueness. This makes you stand out in your field of operation.[16]

19. Divine purpose guarantees focus, concentration and balance, for you to know exactly where you are going and you go for it.

20. Divine purpose is not "*DECIDED* "it is "*DISCOVERED*".

CHAPTER THREE - SUMMARY

The Attributes of Purpose

1.   Your purpose in life is God's sole plan for your life; it is unique or peculiar to you, being enhanced by the purposes of others, having all you need for its fulfillment packaged inside of you.

2.   Divine purpose is more important; powerful and it precedes man's plans.

3.   Therefore, man's plans should be produced from Divine purpose.

REFLECTIONS

1.   How different am I from other people: In what way(s) do I stand out or what am I good at?

2.   In what way have I benefitted or can I benefit from the purposes of others and vice-versa?

3.   What gifts do I possess that makes me stand out?

4.   How can I differentiate my plans from God's purposes for my life?

5.   How much of God's plans for my life have I pursued, compared to my personal desires?

Champions are a rare breed. They trust God while others ask for answers. They step forward while everyone else prays for volunteers. They see beyond the dangers, the risk, obstacles and the hardships.

- Lester Sumrall

4

OPPOSITIONS TO DIVINE PURPOSE

Dr David Oyedepo said, ""**If you give in to opposition, you will lose your position**". This is a warning that many never adhere to, therefore in their pursuit of purpose they end up suffering immense devastation.

Oppositions are hideous enemies that should not be negotiated with but conquered. Their appearance on your path of purpose can blur your vision, slowing you down and ultimately killing your dreams.

Steve Potter said: "**The road to success has many parking places**". So refuse to slow down as you avoid these enemies of purpose.

Fear of Failure:
"**Failure is never final, and success is**

never-ending. Success is a journey not a destination" - *Dr Robert Schuler.*

You need to understand that failure is not the end when you are on the path of purpose. It is only a proof of the fact that some things in your life are to be addressed more intelligently. Being afraid to take steps towards your purpose is like dying a thousand times before death actually comes.

Understand that failing doesn't make you a failure but giving up and accepting your failure, and refusing to try again makes you a failure. You have to do away with the pains of the past, which came as a result of past failures and press on towards the fulfillment of your God ordained purpose[1].

Wrong Association:
Keep Company with the wise and you will become wise. If you make friends with stupid people, you will be ruined. (Proverbs 13:20 GNT).

You need to understand that the kind of company you keep will determine your attitude (thinking pattern) and your attitude determines your altitude (how high you rise in life)[2].

Who you associate with determines your manners and character[3]. Therefore, the person you closely walk with will determine how far you go and ultimately where you end up. You need to choose your friends carefully and wisely. You don't need to know everyone in life, but only the right people.

Some have thrown off caution, wanting to be accepted by their present peer group; they end up being detoured from their path of purpose.

Lack of Information and Exposure:
Form your purpose by asking for counsel, and then carry it out using all the help you can get. (Proverbs 20:18 MSG).
Surprisingly, purposes are defeated when information is lacking. Anyone on the path of purpose without adequate information and proper exposure is like a man scheduled for a boxing match; dressed in a boxing outfit and in the boxing arena but putting on a blindfold.

Such a person's effort is wasted for he becomes myopic and ends up settling for less rather than God's best. Lack of information produces mediocrity. It limits and brings about stagnation.

I have made up my mind to go for information, because to be informed is to be transformed.

Not to be informed is to be deformed. Make your choice.

Sins and Ungodly Habits:
 "The most tragic of all in the long run is the ultimate attitude- it doesn't matter" says Rollo May. Whatever sin or ungodly habit you overlook today will *"over run you tomorrow"*.

The writer of Hebrews admonishes that "we should rid ourselves of every thing that gets in the way, and of the sins which holds on to us tightly, and let us run with determination the race that lies before us"[4].

Sin is a silent killer that destroys faster than any known disease because the latter's power can only be exercised over the physical body but the former has the power to destroy not only the physical body but also to corrupt purpose and ultimately damn a person in Hell. Therefore, its time to break free from all worldly entanglement as you pursue with keen concentration your God-ordained purpose.

Lack of Determination and Confidence:
Please appreciate this fact, that **"your determination determines the reality of your destination"**[5]. Many people just refuse to stay in the game long enough, forgetting

that it is not so important who starts the game, but who finishes it.

Others can stop you temporarily, but you are the only one that can stop yourself permanently. If one advances confidently in the direction of his God given purpose and determines to live the life which he has imagined, he will meet with success unexpectedly in common hours.

Being Satisfied With the Present:
The great inventor Thomas Edison said: **"Show me a thoroughly *satisfied* man and I will show you a failure"**. Being satisfied with your present destroys the zeal to pursue your future because divine purpose is always unfolded in phases. Therefore, a man that resigns to the present has resigned the successive fulfillment of his God-ordained purpose.

Paul the Apostle said: "one thing I do, forgetting those things which are behind and reaching forward to those things which are ahead...."[6].

Understand that your *"today"* is the *"tomorrow"* you spoke about *"yesterday"*[7]. Therefore, break free from the complacency of today and reach out for the reward of purpose that lies ahead.

Refusing To Change:
When you refuse to change, you will end up in chains, but if you subscribe to change, you will take charge of your future, thereby, accomplishing your purpose. Rick Warren said: **"when you are through improving then you're through"**. The truth is that, if you keep doing what you've always done, you will keep getting what you've always got[8]. It is time therefore, to go for change that you might make the needed CHANGE.

Lack of Excellence:
Then God saw everything that he had made, and indeed it was very good (excellent). (Gen 1:31)

> **When you refuse to change, you will end up in chains, but if you subscribe to change, you will take charge of your future...**

We are the offspring of the God of purpose. He pursued His dream of creation having excellence as His hallmark. We are created beings of purpose, carrying a similar potential as our creator, to pursue our purpose.

Therefore, it becomes highly essential that we pursue our purpose with a mark of excellence. Anything short of this is tantamount to a waste of potential, which ends up in a life that lacks fulfillment and satisfaction.

CHAPTER FOUR SUMMARY

Opposition to Divine Purpose
•   Opposition on your path of purpose should not be negotiated with, but conquered. So avoid the following enemies of Divine purpose.
1.   Fear of failure.
2.   Wrong Association.
3.   Lack of Information and Exposure
4.   Sins and Ungodly Habits.
5.   Lack of determination and confidence.
6.   Satisfaction with the present.
7.   Refusing to change.
8.   Lack of Excellence.

REFLECTIONS
1.   In what way have I overlooked certain negative factors that are detrimental to the pursuit of my divine purpose?
2.   What are the oppositions slowing me down presently as I pursue God's divine agenda for my life?
3.   What must I do to avoid or conquer these negative factors on my path of purpose?

Watch out and guard yourselves from every kind of greed: because a person's "true life" is not made up of the things he owns, no matter how rich he may be.

Luke 12:15 GNT

5

FOUNDATION OF
TRUE SUCCESS

The success and solidity of any building can be traced to its foundation. The foundation determines the strength of the building, its height and ultimately its longevity.

Just as the root determines the strength, height and life-span of a plant, so also the foundation of any life can be traced to its singular source. ***Unless the Lord builds the house, they labour in vain who build it. (Ps 127: 1a).***

God is the foundation upon which any life truly succeeds. Now, the first word *"build"* used in the above verse, in the original translation actually means *"ARCHITECTURAL DESIGN"*.

Therefore, we can paraphrase that verse this way: unless the lord gives you *His Architectural design*, your labour will be in vain (useless). No wonder many so-called successful people are fed up with their seemingly successful lives.

They may look gorgeous on the outside but they live a life of frustration on the inside. They have all that anyone could wish for, but they often sense emptiness, or vacuum on the inside.

God is the foundation upon which any life truly succeeds.

Most of these people have dedicated their lives to something they hate doing, just because of the monetary benefit they will make. Some have sought acceptance in a club or a clique, trying to belong yet losing their uniqueness and individuality.

Some people are successful in the world's standard, but every part of their life is going through hell. Their relationship is not working, their children are delinquent, and their spouses are unfaithful.

They keep having one court case after another; sicknesses and diseases keeps ravaging their bodies', etc, yet they fail to realize that it's all because they are disconnected from God, who has the architectural design for the successful construction of their lives.

No matter the elegance of an edifice, if the foundation is faulty, it's only a matter of time before it will collapse. The psalmist says in Psalm 11: 3: *If the foundations are destroyed, what can the righteous do?*

Even the righteous has no answer for a destroyed foundation. Unless you get to know your source and establish a relationship with Him through his son Jesus Christ, you have no hope of a fulfilling and satisfying life, for your acquaintance with God is the foundational key on which true success is achieved.

Give in to God, come to terms with him and everything will turn out just fine. Let him tell you what to do, take his words to heart. Come back to God Almighty and he'll rebuild your life. Clean your house of everything evil. Relax your grip on your money and abandon your gold – plated luxury. God almighty will be your treasure, more wealth than you can imagine. (Job22:21-25 MGS).

SUCCESS IS NOT RICHES

You need to understand that success is not determined by the amount of money a man has, neither by the accumulation of his material possession.

"A person's true life (or success) is not made up of the things he owns, no matter how rich he may be". (Luke 12:15b GNT)

Rather, the success record of anything is determined by its ability to successfully carry out its functions. A product is said to have failed if it fails to fulfill its assignment for which it was made.

A product that successfully accomplishes another function other than its specific function is also considered a failure by its manufacture. Many people are busy doing many other things outside their God ordained mandate.

They may make money, some even become famous, but they never make God happy. What is a man doing in the political arena; just carrying brief-cases from one office to the other when in reality he was *"MANUFACTURED"* by God to lecture in a higher institution of learning?

What is a man doing in the business world, when he was actually created to function as a preacher? No wonder many are frustrated, confused, unfulfilled and unsatisfied in life.

Even as you read this book, it might be possible that your life may be a reflection of what you are reading. You really need to re-evaluate your life and find out if you are actually doing what you were created for.

Riches and material acquisition are meant to be the benefits obtained as you pursue God's original intention for your life. They are not meant to truly determine how successful a man is.

Therefore, your understanding of purpose delivers you from having to live up to the world's expectations. It also delivers you from the present rat race circle and it conditions your life. It gives meaning to your existence because you now know your exact function and you will then start to measure your performance and successes based on the fulfillment of your unique assignment.

> **Your understanding of purpose delivers you from having to live up to the world's expectations**

Note that, you can't pursue your purpose and not be rich and famous.

*A man's gift **or potential which is as a result of his God given purpose**, makes room for him, and brings him before great men"* (Proverb18:16 *emphasis mine*).

CHAPTER FIVE SUMMARY

Foundation of Success
1.   God is the foundation upon which any life truly succeeds.
2.   Success in life should not be determined by the amount of money a man has, neither by the accumulation of material possession, but by the fulfillment of his divine assignment.
3.   Riches and material possessions are meant to be the benefits obtained as you pursue God's original intention for your life.

REFLECTIONS
1.   Is God truly the foundation upon which my life is built?
2.   Do I really derive fulfillment or satisfaction from the material things that I own?

3.   How well am I acquainted with my maker?

4.   Do I always try to impress others rather than be myself?

*When you are born, each
of you has his or her life
purpose.
It's enclosed in you like a tent,
and during your life,
it's your job to set up the tent.*

- Joan Borysenka

6

DISCOVER YOUR PURPOSE

I wrote in one of the earlier chapters that "purpose is not decided but it is discovered". The word discovered, presupposes that divine purpose does not just jump on a man automatically; rather it must be sought after. ***Seek and you will find (discover). Matt 7:7b.***

Therefore it is essential for you to embark on a diligent adventure towards the discovery of your God given purpose.

WHERE DO I START FROM?
To discover purpose is to discover self. You need to know that you are more than what your parents, friends, colleagues, teachers and pastor said about you. In fact, you are more than what the enemy said about you.

Understand that the true value of a product is not determined by the opinion of other products but its manufacture. You and I are *God's products*. He alone knows the scope of your abilities or potentials.

As a matter of fact, your true identity lies with him. To discover yourself you must discover Him *FIRST*.

For in him we live and move and have our being. Acts17:28a

That I may know him. Philippians3:10a

Most ideally, we should understand that man originated from God; therefore, God is our source. We existed in the mind of God even before the world began.

Then God said, "let us make man in our image, according to our likeness; let them have dominion over the fish of the sea, over the birds of the air and over the cattle, over all the earth and over every creeping thing that creeps on the earth. So God created him; male and female he created them. Then God blessed them. Genesis 1:26-28

And the lord God formed man of the dust of the ground and breath into his nostrils the breath of life, and man became a living being. Genesis 2:7

The scenario that played out in Genesis2:7, picture's God releasing the man envisaged within Him into an earth-suit, which He had formed from the dust of the earth, just the same way a manufacturer releases his *"brainchild"* or dream or idea and packages it with physical material to form a tangible product.

It therefore shows that, we are God's products. He alone has the blueprint or manufacturers manual that contains the details of our production[1] and the manual that contains the details of our operation, therefore in our bid to discover who we really are, we need to return to our source; in order that He might hand down to us the original manual that carries the needed information of why we were created.

A product purchased without its operating manual ends up as a mere decoration in the hand of the user, for the operating manual educates the user as to the scope of the products usage, its limits or what it cannot be used for, in order to promote proper function of the product[2].

Now, understand that your purpose from God is the operating manual[3]. Until the operating manual carrying the details of your assignment is handed over to you, you can never really live the kind of life God had originally intended for you.

HOW DO I DISCOVER PURPOSE?

Through "desire" a man having "separated" himself, "seeketh" and intermeddleth with all wisdom". Proverbs 18:1(KJV-emphasis mine).

I will like to paraphrase that verse this way: *"Through desire a man having separated himself seeks to interfere with divine plans and purpose for his life".*

From the scripture above we can deduce three major secrets that guarantee the handing down of Gods plans and purpose for our lives.

1.   **Desire:**
Dr Mike Murdock said, **"The proof of desire is pursuit"**. Your nonchalant attitude towards the discovery and realization of your God-given purpose is a proof that you lack the passion for its discovery.

What you don't *"desire"* you don't *"deserve",* for you will never *possess* what you are *unwilling* to *pursue.* Most people say I don't have a desire? I say create one; and move on towards God's purpose for your life.

2.   Separation:
Separation goes beyond hiding away in an isolated place, but it is the total withdrawal from anything or anyone that robs you of your total focus and sensitivity to the Holy Spirit in your quest to discovering your divine purpose.

Separation reduces distraction and guarantees focus. When you are fully focused on your priorities, you will eliminate confusion. It is time for you to break free from every unnecessary thing competing for your attention, as you give total focus to the realization of your God-ordained purpose.

3.   Pursuit (Seeketh):
The pursuit of divine purpose is the pursuit of God. The purpose of a product cannot be discovered by asking another product, but rather by asking the manufacturer of that product.

God holds the original blueprint to your assignment as I have said earlier. As you seek him diligently, He unfolds his master plan for your life. Now, let us therefore consider other avenues that will help you discover your God-ordained purpose.

➤ **The Place of Prayer**
Prayer is one of your strongest accesses to the Holy Spirit, who is the custodian of God's

secrets[4]. Prayer guarantees a romance with the Spirit of God, whom Jesus says will show you things to come[5].

Anyone that jokes with the place of prayer is like a ship without a compass or a plane without radar. For the place of prayer is a place of revelation.
Call to me and I will answer you. I'll tell you marvelous and wondrous things that you could never figure out on your own. Jeremiah 33: 3 MSG

You need to cherish the place of prayer; for therein God's secret plans for your life are unfolded.

➤ **Stay on the word of God**
By your words, I can see where I'm going; they throw a beam of light on my dark path. Psalm 119:105 MSG

The word of God is not only a certified guide but it also serves as the surest check on our path to destiny. When you stay on the word, through constant studying and meditation, you are guaranteed flawless direction towards your God-ordained purpose.

The entrance of his words gives light[6] and the Bible says .... *God is light[7]* therefore, we can conclude that, the entrance of God's word brings God on the scene, and God on the scene equals purpose discovered.

As we had already said, He (God) has the blueprint for our lives. Yet so many are ignorant of this fact; they prefer rushing over scriptures, just reading one or two Bible verses in a week or in a month. By this shallow Christian attitude they end up confused, running from one so-called 'prophet' to another to receive a revelation on what steps they are to take in life.

Friend, you need not *run around* rather *sit around* the word of God, until a sure path is unfolded to you, as you make your way towards destiny.

> **Waiting**

Isaiah 64: 4 (KJV) says: *For since the beginning of the world, men have not heard nor perceived by the ear, neither hath the eye seen, O God, besides thee what He hath prepared (or purposed) for him that WAITETH for him.*

Divine purpose may sometimes take time before it is received, therefore the need to wait. Waiting is a period wherein you make "enquires"[8] about His plans and purpose for your life.

It is not a time to hurriedly abandon what you are presently doing, but rather it is a state of constant communion with the Holy Spirit. It is a time you wait patiently for His instructions, while you are busy with your present responsibilities.

Doing nothing, taking no steps, hiding away to receive a "Spectacular revelation" from God concerning His purpose is mere wasting of time.

Therefore, get going, yet creating avenues for God to speak always, and God's divine purpose for your life will surely be handed down.

OTHER TIPS TO DISCOVERING YOUR PURPOSE:

Apart from the insights that I had discussed earlier, I would like you right now to take a few minutes and write down your sincere answers to the purpose questions detailed below.

- What do I enjoy doing?
- What am I good at?
- What are my unique gifts or talents?
- What are the things I can do and I have not started doing?
- What would I do gladly without first thinking of the pay?

- What do I do with the least amount of effort (it comes naturally)?
- What are those things I can be persecuted or die for?
- What is it that I do that gives my life the greatest meaning?
- What in my past brings back sweet memories?
- What would I be willing to do if I knew I cannot fail?
- If I were to be given a million Dollars what will I readily spend it on?
- What would I love to do that unlocks my compassion?
- What stirs up anger in me enough for me to do something to fix it?
- What do I want to be remembered for?

Take time to go through and ponder the answers you've written out, then checkout the common factor that keeps showing up in all your answers.

As you patiently carry out this exercise, a picture of your true self will begin to emerge. Your values and legacy will become visible. Go back again to your answers carefully; armed with your new insight, begin to define a purpose or mission statement for your life. Work on this process until you come up with a summarized sentence, revealing in clear terms your purpose or mission statement.

TAKE NOTE OF THESE FOUR QUALITIES OF A GOOD PURPOSE STATEMENT

➤ **Make sure it's scripturally based**: the word of God is the surest check to all issues regarding his divine agenda for our lifes[9].

➤ **Make sure it is short concise and specific**: Nothing becomes dynamic until it becomes specific. I will give you mine as an example......

"My purpose in this life is to reach out to men and women all over the world with the truth of God's word, helping them to discover, enter and fulfill their God ordained destiny".

➤ **Make sure it is transferable**: It can be committed to the memory of others[10].

➤ **Make sure it is measurable**: It must be practical enough to evaluate and to know if you can achieve it.

Understand that it's only a well defined purpose, clearly written out and thoroughly planned out that can be properly pursued.

The Lord gave me this answer. Write down clearly on clay tablets what I reveal to you, so that it can be read at a glance. Habakkuk 2:2, GNT.

If one of you is planning to build a tower, you sit down first and "<u>workout</u>" what it will cost, to see if you have enough money to finish the Job. Luke 14:28, GNT

You need to bring together the various divine revelations concerning your purpose in life as a result of your enquires from God with the various conclusions you arrived at, as a result of our previous questions, and together establish a clear purpose for your life.

Also you'll need to make a list of things and people to do away with, that have no bearing with your God-ordained purpose.

Also, take time out to ask questions, seek for counsel, attend seminars, and listen to CDs relevant to the discovery of your life's purpose.

For as Richard carswell says: "The richest discovery you will ever make is the discovery of who you really are. We must never compromise". We must constantly ask ourselves this simple question, "Are we living out our purpose?"

CHAPTER SIX SUMMARY

Discover your Purpose

1.   To discover purpose is to discover yourself; to discover yourself you have to discover God first.

2.   God alone has the details on why you were created and how you are expected to fulfill your mission here on earth.

3.   Discovering your divine purpose requires strong desire, which eliminates all forms of confusion as you pursue tenaciously God's divine agenda for your life. You need to take time out to seek God in prayer; study God's word and enquire from Him about your purpose.

4.   Take time to give answers to questions that point you to your divine purpose in life. Questions like:

    a.   What am I good at?
    b.   What are my unique gifts?
    c.   What comes naturally to me?
    d.   What can I die for? Etc.

5.   Your divine purpose must be scriptural; specific enough to be delivered in a sentence. It must also be easily remembered and easily evaluated.

REFLECTIONS

1.   Do I really have a desire to know God?

2.   How can I receive from God the blue print or manual for my creation?

3.   What do I do when the realization of my divine purpose is delayed?

*He who has a "why" to live for
can bear almost any "how".*
- Nietzsche

*The privilege of a life time
is being who you are.*
- Joseph Cambell

7

FULFILLING YOUR PURPOSE

Many lives are waiting to be touched through your purpose. Therefore it's high time you break free from your lackadaisical attitude and take a bold step with an unflinching courage towards God's original intention for your life as you lay hold on the power of divine purpose.

I will like to share with you eight cardinal factors that will help you to run with your divine purpose and ultimately fulfill it.

SET GOALS:

"No one ever accomplishes anything of consequence without a goal... Goal setting is the strongest human force for self-motivation"- Paul Myer.

Your goal keeps the desired destination in view, it establishes priorities and builds confidence which produces perseverance and eliminates fear. Goals represent where you want to be.

The poorest of all men is not the one without gold, but without a goal. Life for such a one has no meaning-no reason for living. Robert Backhouse in his book says **"if you aim at nothing you hit it"**.

Every worthwhile goal must posses the following attributes:
- It must be specific
- It must be realistic
- It must be measurable
- It must be balanced
- It must be written out
- It must have a time value.

To actualize your goal considers the following steps.
- Prioritize and write out your goal.
- Keep it constantly in view e.g. you can write it on a piece of paper and stick it on your wall.
- Write out daily, weekly, monthly and yearly goals.

- REAR your goals periodically

R - Review
E - Evaluate
A - And
R - Rewrite

PLANNING:

Is there anyone here, who planning to build a new house, doesn't first sit down and figure the cost so you'll know if you can complete it.   (Luke 14:28, MSG)

Planning is simply thinking ahead. Most people roam through life and then grope in the dark. Planning is a process whereby quality attention is given to details. It's a time wherein you pre-empt possible set back or bottle-necks on your path of purpose ahead of time and proffer possible solutions to them.

During planning, you break down the steps you want to embark upon into goals with deadlines. You prioritize your goals and you think issues through, until you arrive at a logical conclusion. To plan daily gives you a room for life time achievement.

WHY PEOPLE DON'T PLAN

1.   **Mental laziness**: Many are just not willing to task their brain in the art of thinking through issues. This type of laziness is actually the worst kind of laziness because it leads to enormous waste, in both human and capital resources.

The lazy man does not roast (or process) what he took in hunting, but diligence is man's precious possession. (Proverbs 12:27)

Despite the physical exertion experienced during hunting, the man is still considered lazy because he leaves his game to rot, because he is too mentally lazy to process it.

2.   Many don't know how to plan, because they are so disorganized.

3.   Some set their goals too high and, over time, they realize they can't achieve it and they get discouraged.

4.   Some don't plan because they believe the Lord's return is very imminent. Yet the Lord commanded his disciples to do business till he comes[1]

RIGHT ASSOCIATION:

Become wise by walking with the wise; hang out with fools and watch your life fall to pieces. (Proverbs 13: 20 ,MSG)

Understand that the choice of the close friends you keep must be determined by what you see yourself becoming. Good friends will inspire, educate, challenge, motivate, comfort, strengthen and steer you in the right direction.

Your potentials, gifts and qualities will always find expression with the right group of people[2]. Your most valuable friends must be those who do not leave you the way they found you, because your life would have increased in value. Turn away from anyone or every one that corrupts your lifestyle, because they will only drag you backwards[3].

Dr Mike Murdock in his book "the making of a champion" says: **"Those who do not increase you will inevitably decrease you"**, therefore, recognize and eliminate those who bring you backwards in your pursuit of purpose.

TIME MANAGEMENT:

There's opportune time to do things, a right time for everything on the earth. Ecclesiastes 3:1, MSG

Time is God's gift for you to enable you to fulfill your purpose. It's the quantity of our days, which can be measured in seconds, minutes, hours, days and years.

What you do with your time each day will determine what you become per period of time. Therefore, your life's purpose can only be effectively accomplished when it is assigned with time-value for its execution.

It is not about how long you live, but how well you were able to achieve your purpose on earth. Understand also, that time is a God-given resource, which, though it cannot be controlled, can be converted and invested into the productive fulfillment of your life's purpose.

Those who sit and watch time pass are said to be killing time, but the truth is that to kill time is not only to cause murder but suicide, because life runs on the currency of time. Therefore, whosoever wastes time is not only wasting money, as many would say, but is actually wasting life.

How to effectively manage your time

1. Establish what your values are in life. What do you hold dearly as very important, what do you hold so precious to your heart. Find out what you are passionate about that makes you different from others.

2.   Set goals based on your values.
3.   Prioritize your goals.
4.   Make a check list of activities based on your goals, differentiating between urgent and non-urgent activities.
5.   Assign time to each activity.
6.   Guard against time robbers (internal and external time robbers) such as poor attitude, procrastination, indecision, interruptions etc.

DEVELOP COURAGE:

God spoke to Joshua, the Israeli war-lord, and successor of Moses, to be courageous[4] as he journeyed along with the people of Israel towards the fulfillment of Gods purpose for the whole nation.

The Lord emphasized this quality to Joshua as a major ingredient that he couldn't do without as he pursued the fulfillment of God's promises to give the descendants of Abraham the land of Canaan. Joshua's good intentions to obey God would not have been enough with out taking corresponding action.

Note essentially that every action involves-risk taking, only a courageous heart that moves confidently in faith and in the direction of God's plans and purpose for his life, will end up with great success that comes by a developed courage.

EMBRACE MISTAKES:

In your quest to fulfill your purpose in life, understand that you live in an imperfect world with imperfect people and you also are an imperfect person, so mistakes are bound to happen.

Therefore realize that mistakes are signals that draw our attention to the fact that we are not getting it or doing things right and we can then change our course and do things correctly. Therefore, when you make mistakes, just do these three things and move on with your life's purpose.

- Admit it
- Learn from it, and
- Don't repeat it.

DILIGENCE:

Observe people who are good at their work. Skilled workers are always in demand and admired; they don't take a back seat to anyone. Proverbs 22:29

Diligence is really an attitude of consistency in what you do. This leads to a rapid development of skills that advertise your value and relevance. A diligent man can never be stranded in the journey of purpose.

PERSISTENCE:
Rob Gilbert said: "**Quitting is a permanent solution to a temporary situation**".

As you run with purpose, you must develop an attitude of not giving up until you get your desired result. Things may not work out as planned, dare to try again. Refuse to give up so soon, remain persistent until you hit your mark.

I'll encourage you to take the words of Van Crouch to heart. He says: "**Winners are just ex-losers who got mad**". The battle of life belongs to the persistent. The victory will finally go to the one who does not quit! Refuse to let friends or circumstances defeat you.

BE EXCELLENTLY ORIENTED:
Excellence is simply good quality in unusual degree. Excellence is the attitude of always striving for the best in all you do. It is not a destination, rather it is a journey.

Therefore, in your journey for purpose, ensure you aim at improvement on a daily basis. Never settle for mediocrity but strive to get better and better everyday.

When excellence becomes your lifestyle, you don't ask how much it will cost, but rather, it becomes necessary to inquire what the cost to attain excellence is.

SEEK THE HELP OF THE HOLY SPIRIT: You must not toil with your connection with God. For every believer, your connection with God is the Holy Spirit who is also called "The comforter" or "Helper"[5]

You need to seek "The Helper" who is the Holy Spirit, if you want your purpose actualized.

Ways to obtain the help of the Holy Spirit

- Acknowledge the person and assignment of the Holy Spirit always.
- Be filled with the Holy Spirit[6].
- Receive the impartation of his wisdom; understanding; counsel; might; knowledge and the fear of God[7].
- Receive and yield to the gifts of the Holy Spirit[8].
- Pay the price for his precious anointing upon your life[9].

CHAPTER SEVEN SUMMARY

Fulfilling your purpose
- Many lives are waiting to be touched by your divine purpose, therefore you have to

give total attention to the following factors:
1.   Set goals.
2.   Planning.
3.   Right Association.
4.   Time Management.
5.   Developing courage.
6.   Embrace mistakes.
7.   Diligence.
8.   Persistence.
9.   Excellence

REFLECTIONS

1.   Do I plan and set worthwhile goals for my life consistently?

2.   If no, can I say I am mentally lazy; disorganized or just ignorant of God's expectations for my life?

3.   Do I have unfulfilled goals?

4.   What can I do to realize my goals in life?

5.   How can I effectively manage my time on a daily basis?

6.   Do I give up easily on negative situations?

7.   How do I receive Help from God to fulfill my divine purpose?

*The most pathetic person
in the world is someone who
has sight but has no vision.*
- Helen Keller

8

COMING SOON

Coming soon? Yes! Coming soon! So was the answer of the security man to this inquisitive pedestrian, who was amused by the picture of a beautiful architectural master piece, erected in front of a dilapidated site with a mighty inscription on the picture boldly displaying the words "COMING SOON"!

Not understanding the connection between the site, picture and inscription he shook is head and straight away took his leave.

YOU ARE COMING SOON!

Just as the picture carried the future beauty and glory of the wasted site, so God has also painted a glorious picture of "you", which is a true reflection of his plan and purpose for your life. This picture also carries an invisible inscription titled "coming soon", though your life is still in its wasted or inferior state.

Your life might be dilapidated or dilapidating right now, you may be despised and rejected, not appreciated nor celebrated. You might have been left out of the club and not welcomed in the clique. I have good news for you: *"You are coming soon"*.

Your mourning would be turned into dancing
Your penury to plenty
Your shame to fame
Your pain to gain
Your obstacles to miracle

For God's purpose for your life is about to burst forth. It's coming with an awesome power, not only to change you, but also to bring about a radical transformation of your immediate environment and ultimately your generation.

Therefore, you can't afford to throw in the towel, for it's too soon to quit, you just have to stay on in the game, for it's not over yet, something "new" is about to happen in your life as you lay hold on power of divine purpose.

REPLAY CLIPS
From the very beginning telling you what the ending will be, all along letting you in

on what is going to happen, assuring you, I'm in this for the long haul, I'll do exactly what, I set out to do. (Isaiah 46:10MSG)

God only speaks when He, has already finished[1]. God does not start before he finishes, rather He finishes before He starts. Then He goes back to the "start" to declare the "finish". Christ's death was already a foregone conclusion even before God's promise of the Messiah (the seed of the woman)[2].

> **Vision is the picture of a finished future revealed in the Now but settled in the PAST**

Everything God is doing presently in your life are *"replay clips"*. They had already taken place. They are only "coming soon" to take place in the now.

SEE YOUR PURPOSE

Whatever God has inscribed over your life is called His "counsel"[3] or translated as His "purpose". God's purpose cannot be changed or altered by any person or any devil[4].

This counsel or purpose He further inscribes in your heart in form of "VISION". Vision is

God's way of giving us a glimpse of His purpose for our lives. "Vision is the picture of a finished future revealed in the Now but settled in the PAST".

Vision is so important to your "coming soon" because you can only actualize the future plan and purpose of God for your life by what you are presently *"seeing"*.

Without the beautiful picture before the dilapidated site, the condition of the site remains the same.

The picture informs the builders of what to do and the steps to take, so also, what you see on the inside affects what you think[5], and what you think affects who you are[6], and who you are affects what you can do (i.e. your strength[7]).

Therefore, your *"picture"* will affect your *"future*; *your "sight"* will affect your *height"*; *your "perception "will affect your "possession"*.

Whatever vision of your divine purpose you are seeing presently is programmed to come at a certain season. Though, it may be delayed, yet it will not be denied[8].

Though it doesn't look like it right now, it is coming soon in a matter of time. Tell yourself,

I am only passing through this phase; it is not my parking space. I'm better than what anyone sees me to be today.

> **For my best days have not been preserved by my past, but they are reserved for my future**

For my best days have not been preserved by my past, but they are reserved for my future, beneath this heap of rubbish lays his purpose for my life waiting to be revealed and subsequently fulfilled.

I pray that you will not only discover, but rather pursue tenaciously, God's will for your life, following the path He has marked out for you, despite all conflicting circumstance, because every negative situation in your life is subject to change.

Your coming soon will be guaranteed as you wholeheartedly lay hold on the POWER OF DIVINE PURPOSE.

CHAPTER EIGHT SUMMARY

Coming Soon

1.   No matter the situation of your life; as long as you hold on to your God ordained purpose, your situation is bound to change for the better.

2.	Your life is really a finished script, even though you are presently living it out.

3.	The vision of your divine purpose that you are able to see connects your present to your glorious tomorrow.

REFLECTIONS
1.	What can I say about my present state?

2.	What do I see about my future?

3.	Am I ready to wait patiently for the fulfillment of my divine purpose?

EPILOGUE

REVIVAL OF PURPOSE

We are at the verge of the most dramatic revival. God is gathering his choicest weapons for a final onslaught on the forces of evil. This is the glory age of the Church of Jesus Christ. God is poised to do extraordinary things through ordinary men.

That's not new, you might say, but I bet you, you haven't heard this: we are already experiencing this move! Friend, the revival we have long awaited for has started. If only you will stop and take your eyes away from the negative circumstances and the unpleasant reports that fly around concerning the church of God, you'll notice a gradual but calculated assembling of an army.

This army is strange; the set up is completely beyond human ability. In fact the book of the prophet Joel[1] reports the army as a company of great people, possessing supernatural strength and stressing their uniqueness.

For their kind had never existed before, never will there be any like them ever again. The beauty of this army is encapsulated in the writings of the prophet Joel. It says: ***They run like mighty men, they climb the wall like men of war; everyone marches in formation, and they do not break ranks. They do not push one another; everyone marches in his own column; though they lunge between the weapons? They are not cut down[2].***

These verses do not only reflect the organized state of the army but they also show that the army is well patterned.

Each soldier has a specific position to occupy and this proper positioning guarantees the preservation of each individual soldier.

The Bible says: *They do not push one another; everyone marches in his OWN COLUMN[3] (i.e. Purpose).*

This is nothing but God's organized army of "PURPOSE POWERED SOLDIERS". These are men and women that have discovered their purpose in life and are purposefully pursuing it with all determination. They are

God's end time "TIME" bombs programmed to detonate at their due season, bringing about definite change in their scope of influence.

Friend! We are right in the middle of an historical "event" invented by God Himself, wherein He is reviving again his original intention for His saints.

It is time to brace up; the best of God awaits anyone and everyone that will press on to lay hold on the POWER OF DIVINE PURPOSE.

YOU'RE NOT AN ACCIDENT

Your birth was no mistake. Though your parents never planned your conception, God did. Long before you were conceived in your mother's womb, you were conceived in the mind of God.

God prescribed every single detail of your body. He deliberately choose your race, the colour of your skin, your hair, and other features that you possess. He also determined the natural talents you would possess and the uniqueness of your personality.

God made you for a reason; nothing in your life is by chance, your past defeats, regrets, disappointments or mistakes notwithstanding. He orchestrated them all for His purpose.

Now consider this, assuming there was no God, we would all be ACCIDENTS! The result of astronomical random chance in the universe, as some would want us to believe.[1]

In fact reading this book would have been a colossal waste of time and resources, and it will be fair to conclude that there is no purpose to life.

The good news however is that God certainly exist, and He made you for a definite purpose and your life has a profound meaning. You will only discover your divine purpose when you make God the reference point of your life.

This you can do by making a decision today to surrender your life to Jesus Christ, the only way that God has made available for all to reach Him[2].

If you're tired of going round in a vicious cycle of confusion and despair, and you want God to open up to you the reason for your existence, please say this out loud:

O Lord, thank you for creating me for a purpose. I recognize and admit that I am a sinner, by my nature and action. I believe that Jesus died for my sins and he rose again on the third day. Lord forgive my sins, as I turn away from SIN today, to live a life pleasing unto you. Thank you for saving me. Amen.

For further enquiries and prayers for your spiritual growth, contact us @

ETERNAL GLORY ASSEMBLY INTERNATIONAL CHURCH

13 Irawo Ogo Jesu/street, Pipeline B/stop, Ishasi road, Akute.
Helpline: +2348029591841; 2348029517135; 2348037915926
Email: eternalgloryassembly@gmail.com

OUR MAIN FELLOWSHIP DAYS
Sundays: 8:00am-9:00am
9:05am-11:00am
Wednesdays: 6:30pm-8:00pm

Ega...Welcome to significance

ENDNOTES

INTRODUCTION
1.   William V. Crouch, Staying Power (Motivational insight to help you stay in the game).

CHAPTER 1
1.   Oxford Advanced learner's dictionary, Photosynthesis- the process by which green plants turn carbon-dioxide and water into food using energy from the sun.
2.   Genesis 1:26 NKJV
3.   Genesis 2:19-20 NKJV
4.   Genesis 2:21-22 NKJV

CHAPTER 2
1.   Romans 8:28 NKJV
2.   Isaiah 46:10 NKJV
3.   Romans 8:30 NKJV
4.   1 Corinthians 5:1-2 NKJV
5.   Acts 19:21 AMP
6.   Philippians 3:13-14 NKJV
7.   1 Sam 16 &22; 2 Sam 23:8 NKJV
8.   1 Corinthians 4:3-5 NKJV
9.   Acts 26:19 NKJV
10.   1 Timothy 6:6-10 NKJV
11.   Hebrews 12:2 NKJV
12.   John 2:13-17 NKJV
13.   Ephesians 1:11 LB
14.   Isaiah 55:8-9 NKJV
15.   Zig-ziglar, Dallas-Texas

CHAPTER 3

1. Eternal Glory Assembly flier 2010, YOU ARE NOT AN ACCIDENT!
2. John 1:19-37 NKJV
3. Proverbs 19:21a NKJV
4. Proverbs 19:21a NKJV
5. Proverbs 19:21b NKJV
6. Proverbs 19:21b NKJV
7. Proverbs 19:21c NKJV
8. Proverbs 19:21c NKJV
9. Proverbs 19:21c NKJV
10. Isaiah 46:10 NKJV
11. Isaiah 46:11 NKJV
12. Isaiah 46:11 NKJV
13. John 21:18, Acts18:9-10 NKJV
14. Acts 26:14-20 NKJV
15. Acts 1:15-26, Rev 3:11 NKJV
16. 2 Peter 3:15-16 NKJV

CHAPTER 4

1. Philippians 3:13-14 NKJV
2. Zig-Ziglar, Dallas-Texas
3. 1 Corinthians 15:33 NKJV
4. Hebrews 12:1 GNT
5. Olatunji Shobayo- Souls Aflame Ministries International, Lagos-Nigeria
6. Philippians 3:13b NKJV
7. Pastor Tunde Bakare, Latter Rain Assembly-Ogba, Lagos-Nigeria
8. Peter Francisco (Staying Power - Van Crouch)

CHAPTER 6

1.   Psalm 139:14-17 NKJV
2.   Romans 8:28 NKJV
3.   Psalm 127:1, Hebrews 3:4 NKJV
4.   1 Corinthians 2:9-12 NKJV
5.   John 16:13 NKJV
6.   Psalm 119:130 NKJV
7.   1 John 1:5b NKJV
8.   Habakkuk 2:1-2 NKJV
9.   Psalm 19:7b; 2Peter 1:19 KJV
10.   1 Timothy 2:2 NKJV

CHAPTER 7

1.   Luke 19:13 NKJV
2.   Proverbs 27:17 GNT
3.   1 Corinthians 15:33 NKJV
4.   Joshua 1:6&7-9 NKJV
5.   John 14:16-17&26 NKJV
6.   John 7:37-39 NKJV
7.   Isaiah 11:2 NKJV
8.   1 Corinthians 12:7-11 NKJV
9.   1 Samuel 16:13 &Luke 4:18 NKJV

CHAPTER 8

1.   Romans 4:17 NKJV
2.   Revelation 13:8 &Genesis 3:15 NKJV
3.   Isaiah 46:10 NKJV
4.   Isaiah 46:11 NKJV
5.   Lamentation 3:51a NKJV
6.   Proverbs 23:7a NKJV
7.   Judges 8:21b NKJV
8.   Habakkuk 2:2 NKJV

EPILOGUE
1.   Joel 2:2 NKJV
2.   Joel 2:7-8 MSG
3.   Joel 2:8b NKJV

YOU'RE NOT AN ACCIDENT
1.   Psalm 14: 1 NKJV
2.   Acts 4: 12 NKJV

THE GRASSHOPPER COMPLEX:

This book gives you access to time proven principles that will help you go beyond your challenges and help you each out for God's promises that lies ahead

UNDERSTANDING DIVINE OPEN DOORS:

In this book, learn what it takes to escape the trap of settling for less rather than God's best.

In this book, learn what it takes to escape the trap of settling for less rather than God's best.

BORN TO LEAD:
This book unveils the truth behind God's leadership mandate for every man, and it explains succinctly how leadership can be properly utilized.

...caution: these books are dangerous to your ignorance!

You can purchase and help distribute any of these books. For enquiry, please call +234-802-959-1841

SOULS AFLAME **MINISTRIES INTERNATIONAL**

....helping you fulfil destiny

The Souls Aflame Ministries International was inaugurated on the 27th of October, 2001. The vision was borne out of a passion to reach out to men and women all over the world with the truth of God's word to the end that they might discover, enter, and fulfil their God ordained destinies.

The organization headed by Olatunji Olubayo intends to raise an army of purpose driven men and women in the society, having a strong drive towards their destiny, with excellence and integrity as their hallmark.

This outstanding organization achieves its aim through the following outfits:

*   *ETERNAL GLORY ASSEMBLY INTERNATIONAL CHURCH (EGA).*
*   *SOULS AFLAME GLOBAL OUTREACH (SAGLO).*
*   *SOULS AFLAME MEDIA OUTREACH (SAMO).*
*   *EXCEL PUBLISHING HOUSE (EPH)*
*   *LIFE AND MINISTRY DEVELOPMENT INSTITUTE-(a.k.a GLORY BIBLE INSTITUTE).*
*   *MISSIONS AWARENESS INITIATIVE (MAIN)*

PARTNERS AFLAME INTERNATIONAL

Invitation to Partnership

For the purpose of achieving the aforementioned vision, you are invited to partner with us under the umbrella of PARTNERS AFLAME INT'L.

As our partner, you occupy a special position and you also play a strategic role in the fulfilment of this vision. Your commitment is vital, valuable and important.

Your connection and participation in this unique vision will open you up to the divine ability to fulfil God's unique purpose for your life. As you partake of God's unique grace and His divine covering through this commission, over your life and family.

HOW TO GET INVOLVED

- ***PRAY FOR US**- Pray for the Leadership and all arms of the ministry.*
- ***PAY FOR US**- Help us meet the enormous bills involved in running this ministry, through your financial support. We in turn pray for you and yours, believing God for an hundred fold return on every seed sown.*

For more information on Ministry activity, and how you can become a financial partner, please visit:

www.soulsaflame.org
Email:sam_intl2002@yahoo.co.uk
olatunjishobayo@yahoo.com
eternalgloryassembly@gmail.com
Tel: +234-802-959-1841, 234-803-474-3878, 234-809-859-1841

ABOUT THE AUTHOR

Olatunji Olubayo is the dynamic and charismatic founder of Souls Aflame Ministries International, a multifaceted ministry in the outskirts of Lagos city.

A graduate of Agricultural Bio-chemistry and Nutrition from the University of Ibadan, where he held Leadership positions at different levels in the Student Christian Movement between 1991 and 1995. He is currently the general secretary of PFN Ojodu Chapter, Lagos- Nigeria.

He is presently the Senior Pastor of Eternal Glory Assembly International Church with a mandate to raise a people driven and powered by divine purpose, having excellence and integrity as their distinctive features.

Through his vibrant itinerant outreaches, he is much sought after as a speaker in conferences, conventions, seminars, crusades both in churches and campuses.

His message of Purpose, Hope, and Destiny cuts across a wide spectrum of human need, catapulting his listeners into their God ordained destinies.

He is the author of the much sought after book, **THE POWER OF DIVINE PURPOSE** *and the CEO of Excel Publishing House, an outfit committed to publishing the mission with passion.*

He is married to the delectable Oluwaseyi Adetutu, a graduate of Ammadu Bello University Zaria with masters in Business Administration (MBA) and his life long companion in ministry.

They have the privilege of parenting their two lovely kids- David and Vanessa.

9 789789 178476